NEW YORK

A Photographic Journey

TEXT: **Bill Harris**

CAPTIONS: **Fleur Robertson**

DESIGNED BY: **Teddy Hartshorn**

EDITORIAL: **Gill Waugh and Jane Adams**

PRODUCTION: **Ruth Arthur and David Proffit**

DIRECTOR OF PRODUCTION: **Gerald Hughes**

DIRECTOR OF PUBLISHING: **David Gibbon**

CLB 2445
© 1989 Colour Library Books Ltd., Godalming, Surrey, England.
All rights reserved.
This 1989 edition published by Crescent Books,
distributed by Crown Publishers, Inc., 225 Park Avenue South, New York, New York 10003.
Printed and bound in Hong Kong.
ISBN 0 517 00176 4
h g f e d c b a

NEW YORK

A Photographic Journey

Text by
BILL HARRIS

CRESCENT BOOKS
NEW YORK

Part of the decoration in the lobby of the Empire State Building in New York City consists of illustrations of the Seven Wonders of the World at the time of Alexander the Great. When the building was finished in 1931 it was widely hailed as the eighth wonder of the world, but students of antiquity knew that the natural successor to the original seven had already been a part of the New York scene since 1886. And of the many dreams that are the fabric of New York, nothing is more symbolic of them than the statue that stands in the harbor, Frederic-Auguste Bartholdi's *Liberty Enlightening the World*.

One of the ancient Wonders, the Colossus of Rhodes, also overlooked one of the world's great harbors and was placed there as a symbol of the spirit and creativity of a nation. It was also remembered for centuries as the biggest and best of the great colossal statues. But it was a full fifty feet shorter than the lady in New York harbor. Even Nero's spectacular monument to himself in Rome was thirty feet shorter. The Statue of Liberty, from the tip of her toe to the top of her torch, is 151 feet, one inch high. Along with the pedestal, the whole monument rises to a height of 305 feet, six inches.

Since October 28, 1886 when President Grover Cleveland officially accepted this gift of the people of France, the statue has consistently been among New York's top five tourist attractions and, except for the Brooklyn Bridge, which predates it by five years and three months, it is the oldest landmark synonymous with the city itself.

But the Statue of Liberty is more than a symbol of New York City. It is a landmark of the American dream. And it stands less than a half mile away from the second greatest landmark of the same dream, Ellis Island.

The immigrant station at Ellis Island was formally opened on January 1, 1892 when a transfer boat carrying 148 steerage passengers from the S.S. *Nevada* pulled in to its new pier. Annie Moore, a fifteen year-old girl from Ireland was first to set foot on the island as an immigrant. Before it was closed as a reception center in 1932, more than sixteen million souls had followed in her footsteps.

In its final year the Ellis Island facility processed 21,500 immigrants. In its peak year, 1907, 1,285,349 were admitted.

During World War II and up until its final closing in 1954, Ellis became a detention and deportation center and some German aliens were held prisoner there, in the shadow of the Statue of Liberty, for all of the war years. It was possibly because of that final bitter memory that the Eisenhower Administration declared the island surplus in 1956 and offered it for sale to the highest bidder. The announcement at least had the sensitivity to refer to it as "one of the most famous landmarks in the world".

None of the bids and proposals proved high enough. The highest was an offer of close to two million dollars offered by a New York developer who wanted to build a mini-city on the twenty-seven-and-a-half-acre island and had even provided designs by the great American architect Frank Lloyd Wright.

Such proposals were laid to rest in 1965 when President Lyndon B. Johnson proclaimed Ellis Island and the Statue of Liberty partners in a national monument. His proclamation included plans for restoration which have yet to be realized.

Almost two decades later, a new Administration in Washington with strong faith in "the private sector" decided ordinary citizens should contribute the money necessary to do the job as well as fund desperately needed repair work on the Statue of Liberty herself.

It's not an unprecedented request. The Statue was built with funds donated by French citizens, but the million francs they raised wasn't enough to build a base for it in New York. A subscription drive on this side of the Atlantic produce enough to build fifteen feet of masonry, but the Statue was doomed to stay in 214 crates in a Paris warehouse for more than a year while Joseph Pulitzer used the editorial page of his *New York World* to convince New York citizens that their pennies and dimes mattered in making this part of the dream come true.

The Island of Manhattan across the Bay has been a symbol of dreams since Henry Hudson first took word of it back to the Dutch East India Company in 1609. "It is as beautiful a land as one can hope to tread upon," he told them. With typical Dutch caution, it took them four more years to send Adriaen Block to see if Hudson was telling the truth. It took them another eight years to change their name to the Dutch West India Company and declare the territory their private preserve.

Their original settlement was on present-day Governor's Island. But the way Washington Irving's Diedrich Knickerbocker tells the tale, they missed the point and put their first settlement in the New Jersey swamps. If you take his word for it, that's where the great city would be today if a party of explorers led by Oloffe Van Kortlandt had not been shipwrecked on the western shore of the East River about where the end of 89th Street is today, the spot where the Mayor's official residence, Gracie Mansion, is located. And according to Father Knickerbocker, they'd have gone home completely unimpressed had not Van Kortlandt dreamed a dream.

"... And, lo, the good St. Nicholas came riding over the tops of the trees in that self-same wagon wherein he brings his yearly presents to children," wrote Irving in his description of Oloffe's vision. "The shrewd Van Kortlandt knew him by his broad hat, his long pipe and the resemblance he bore to the figure on the bow of the Goede Vrouw (the ship which had brought them to the New World). And he lit his pipe by the fire and he sat himself down and smoked; and as he smoked the smoke from his pipe ascended into the air and spread like a cloud overhead. And the sage Oloffe hastened and climbed up to the top of one of the tallest trees, and saw that the great volume of smoke spread over a great extent of country – and as he considered it more attentively, he fancied that the great volume of smoke assumed a variety of marvelous forms, where in dim obscurity he saw shadowed-out palaces and domes and lofty spires, all of which lasted a moment, and the whole rolled off and nothing but the green woods were left. And when St. Nicholas had smoked his pipe he twisted it in his hatband, and laying a finger beside his nose he gave the astonished Van Kortlandt a very significant look; then mounting his wagon he returned over the treetops and disappeared."

When the explorers got back to their settlement across the Hudson, their fellow citizens agreed that St. Nicholas indeed intended them to settle the Island of Manhattan and that Van Kortlandt was ".... a most useful citizen and a right good man – when he was asleep."

The truth is that the merchants in New Amsterdam didn't need a dream to convince them that there were riches beyond their own wildest dreams waiting for them on this tiny island. In 1626 they dispatched Peter Minuit with instructions to buy the place. The deal was made in front of a fort the Dutch were building at the present-day site of the Custom House on Bowling Green. The price was sixty Guilders, well known in today's money as twenty-four dollars. The deal has often been referred to as one of the slickest real estate transactions in history. But two years later, Minuit paid roughly the same price to the same Indian tribe for all of Staten Island. Manhattan is 14,211 acres, compared to Staten Island's area of 36,600 acres. Three years after that the Dutch fired Peter Minuit for being overly-generous and he went into the service of the Swedish Government, on whose behalf he bought most of Delaware, including the present site of Wilmington, for one copper pot.

But if New York has always been a mecca for opportunists, it has been important from the very beginning to the dreams of people looking for opportunity. The Dutch settled their colony here with refugees from Belgium who had migrated to Holland looking for religious freedom and, having found it, then wanted more in the way of financial betterment. Dutch was the official language of New Amsterdam, but before its population reached 500 it was reported that eighteen different languages were spoken there.

That was just the beginning.

By the end of the seventeenth century, the English had taken over but the Dutch didn't move away. The result was that New York became America's first truly international city and the stage was set to make it a key element in what would soon become known as "the American dream."

When the Dutch moved to America their basic goal was what historians call economic opportunity. They came to make money. When the English took over their idea was essentially the same. Until the Revolutionary War, Boston had been, along with Philadelphia, the major port of entry for merchandise exported by the great British merchants. Unfortunately for them, both Boston and Philadelphia suffered a bad press in England during the war years. But New York was in British hands during most of those years and when it was all over it became the favored port of the English merchant fleets. By 1815, the value of imports coming into New York Harbor was more than double that of Boston and three times that of Philadelphia.

At the same time New York became established as the best

place for immigrants to head for, simply because there were more jobs there. Then, ten years later, in 1825, the Erie Canal connected New York with the riches of the West. From that moment on, New York could truly be called a city of many dreams.

An immigrant who put his dream to work in a spectacular way was a young man who arrived here from Waldorf, Germany, in 1784. His name was John Jacob Astor. He married a local girl a year later and used his bride's dowry to get into the fur business. By the beginning of the new century he had already amassed a fortune of a quarter of a million dollars, some of which he used to get into the China trade. He sent his ships from New York around the tip of South America to Oregon, where he had established a colony he modestly called Astoria. They went to China from there loaded with furs from the Pacific Northwest and completed the circle by coming back to New York loaded down with tea and silk. In the process Astor became the richest man in New York City. By 1840 he was known around town as "New York's landlord," with 355 pieces of property, all fully rented.

In 1850, two years after Astor died, P.T. Barnum paid the unheard-of rent of $500 a week for Castle Garden, the converted fortress at the edge of Battery Park, to introduce his latest "discovery," the Swedish soprano Jenny Lind.

By today's standards it was a low price. The theater could seat 6,000, only a handful less than the capacity of Radio City Music Hall, the biggest theater in the world today. But it was a fortune to Barnum, who announced he would hold an auction for tickets to the Swedish Nightingale's opening night. The auction, held in Castle Garden, was attended by 5,000 people, each of whom had paid a "bit" (half a quarter) for the privilege of being there. Only one thousand tickets were auctioned but Barnum collected $10,141 for his afternoon's work. Many of the people who put in successful bids turned a nice profit, too. The event gave birth to an institution that has existed ever since. The tickets were resold by these first scalpers in the park outside on opening day.

All the greats of the world of entertainment appeared at Castle Garden during its years as a theater, from songwriter Stephen Foster to dancer Lola Montez. It was the scene of band concerts and operas, political rallies and Shakespearean productions, variety shows and important debates.

Then, on August 3,1855, Castle Garden became America's first reception center for immigrants. In the next thirty-five years and eight months, 7,690,606 would pass through the doors of the former theater, an average of eighteen hundred a month. In the days before the Civil War, nearly all of the immigrants arrived in sailing ships and the vast majority of them had little stomach for traveling any further once they got to New York, in spite of the common advice in Europe that they should avoid the cities once they arrived in America.

In the thirty years before New York opened that formal immigration reception center, the city's population had grown from 166,000 to 630,000. And it had long since taken on the cosmopolitan attitude it has never lost. In the 1830s a visiting European was astounded to find strolling along Broadway: "people of color, Germans and Dutch, Irish, French, Danes, Swiss, Welsh, English, Scots, Italians, Turks, Chinese, Swedes, Russians, Norwegians, Poles, Hungarians, Spaniards, Sicilians, Africans and, in short, a few of all the nations upon the earth."

Castle Garden has taken back its original name, Castle Clinton, and is now, like Ellis Island and the Statue of Liberty, a national monument. But there are other, less formal, memorials to the immigrants, many of which still serve the immigrants of today: the tenements of the Lower East Side.

New arrivals to New York in the nineteenth century generally spent their first nights in boarding houses near the docks. Often whole families were packed into a single room. Ideally, the arrangement was only temporary and as soon as they were able they moved on to more permanent quarters. But in some cases they went from bad to worse.

The huge waves of Irish immigrants who arrived in the 1840s moved into an area at the western edge of today's Chinatown. Their community of run-down buildings, including an abandoned brewery, and tar paper shacks, was known as Five Points. Charles Dickens said of it, "... debauchery has made the very houses prematurely old." It was an area controlled by violent street gangs whose victims were lucky if they could get away with nothing more than having an ear or a nose bitten off or an eye deftly gouged out. In later years, Al Capone bragged that nothing in Chicago was a match for him because he had grown up in Five Points.

As soon as they could, the Irish moved slightly east and north into the areas that are called Chinatown and Little Italy these days. They left their former homes to the Germans and Poles, English and Italians who followed them to the New World.

Among the newer arrivals, the Germans were the first to pick up stakes and move on. They moved into the area north of City Hall and south of 14th Street, known today as the Lower East Side. In the 1850s their presence gave it the name "Klein-Deutschland," Little Germany. They held sway there until after the turn of the century, giving up only the portion of their territory below Houston Street to the waves of Jewish immigrants who were beginning to arrive from Russia and Romania. The quarter became almost all Jewish after the Germans began moving uptown above 83rd Street (displacing the Irish, by the way) after the first subway was built in 1904.

Ironically, the uptown neighborhood, called Yorkville, is commonly thought of as a German community; the Lower East Side is considered Jewish. But neither of them could the claim the label until only seventy-five years ago.

The second generations of immigrant families didn't feel the need to cling to their own ethnic groups and dispersed elsewhere, leaving the old ghetto-like neighborhoods to other new arrivals. The first waves moved away from Manhattan and into the other Boroughs of New York City and though many of them are raising their children there today, they are increasingly surrounded by people who, like their grandparents, find the English language bewildering and the American way of life the object of a dream that's difficult to grasp.

And, like the earlier immigrants, this new wave, the biggest since the 1920s, seeks the companionship of people who speak their language and share their customs. Immigrants from mainland China have expanded the borders of Chinatown to the consternation of the people across Canal Street in Little Italy where signs in shop windows are more and more likely to be Chinese ideograms, and the restaurants are as likely to feature lemon chicken as chicken cacciatore. New arrivals from the Middle East or from the Caribbean are likely to find a touch of home in

Brooklyn. But among the new ethnic outposts, the one that outdoes them all is a little community in Queens not far from La Guardia Airport that provided escape from the city for the English and Dutch in Colonial times, the neighborhood called Elmhurst.

At the beginning of 1982, the U.S. Immigration and Naturalization Service reported that there were 650,000 legal immigrants living in the five Boroughs of New York City. On top of that, city agencies estimate that there are 750,000 aliens living in New York who got here by other than legal means and therefore are not counted in official tallies. All of them have one thing in common: the famous American dream. They're here to make it big and some of them will. Meanwhile, just "making it" is the order of the day.

Out in Elmhurst, a cop on the beat says "... anything God put on this earth, we've got two of them right here in the ll0th Precinct." And at Public School 89, whose 1,600 young students were born in fifty different countries, only about a third of the kids will tell they are "American" rather than Korean, Columbian or Yugoslavian; but almost none will say they'd like to go back to where they were born. "It's better over here," says one, '"we've got sports, video games, movies." Their parents know they've got much more and that, by and large, is why they're here with a dream and a desire. And why they probably will never go back.

But New York attracts more than just immigrants and ordinary job-hunters. Even though the unemployment rate among young people is higher in New York than in some other parts of the country and increasing numbers of people have been leaving the cities of the Northeast for the climate and opportunities in the Southwest, there's a segment of the population of America that knows the only way to make their fondest dreams come true is to come to New York.

Their average age is twenty-two to twenty-nine years old. They're college-educated. They're eager, even excited. And over the past fifteen years they've migrated to New York in increasing numbers, making themselves one of the fastest-growing segments of the City's population and giving New York America's biggest net increase in citizens of that age group.

Traditionally, young people migrating to New York have been aspiring actors and artists, musicians and writers. And they're still arriving every day of the week. But in the last few years, more and more young people have been coming to New York in search of a business career. Some of them are young lawyers, others have fresh MBA diplomas tucked into their briefcases. Often as not they'll say that they chose New York not just because there are better jobs for them here, but because the on-the-job training they'll get will make them more valuable back where they came from.

But when they get here, something strange happens. They themselves provide a spark to the New York atmosphere that no other city has. Then the spark turns to fire and before you know it, they're hooked. Peoria never ever looks that attractive again.

Obviously, one of the things that makes New York so attractive to them is the other people in the same age group they meet and share their dreams with. An artist who came to experiment, an actor who works part-time as a waiter to give him more time to go to auditions and classes, a music student who makes ends meet by giving impromptu recitals on a Fifth Avenue street corner, all have one very important thing in common: each other. They find the diversity exhilarating, too. They give New York a huge measure of its vitality and excitement and that's precisely what they came here to find, not to mention what keeps them here.

But if there is so much dreaming going on in New York, why is everyone so wide awake? Probably the best reason is because so many of those dreams are coming true. It's possible to be successful in places like Los Angeles or Chicago, of course, but there's a certain pride that goes along with being a success in New York that makes it something special. Though people on the way up will usually tell you that this kind of pride is the prize they're after, you know that's about the same as a student who says he's after a medical degree because he wants to help people.

The thing that makes the world go around in New York is money, and there are more ways to make more of it than just about any other spot on earth. In earlier generations, the road to success was usually paved on the playing fields of the right schools and in quiet recesses of the right clubs. But these days, more often than not, the key to success is being in the right place at the right time. The right place right now happens to be New York.

It's a place where two people can bump into each other on the street and in less than five minutes change the direction of their lives. It's a place where a young person can get noticed, where new ideas can get accepted. If Horatio Alger were alive today, his stories would have to be about New Yorkers.

The reason why it all works is because there are so many people working at it. There are more than 23,000 people per square mile in New York, and that's just those who live here. The Monday-Friday working environment is so densely packed with people who commute from every direction to jobs in New York that on weekends, when the suburbanites all stay home, the people who live in New York feel almost lonely.

On weekends they worry less about "gridlock" – that threatened menace traffic experts predict will happen on the day when crosstown traffic blocks all the up and downtown intersections and everybody just gets out of their car and walks away. They don't worry at all about finding parking places, which is much easier on Saturdays and Sundays, because Manhattanites, at least, quite unlike any other segment of the American population, don't own cars. Insurance rates are higher, monthly parking costs more than two-bedroom apartments in other cities and the average speed of traffic on weekdays is under ten miles an hour. Besides, when you live in New York, where else is there to go?

That's not to say Manhattanites are homebodies. There are probably more telephone answering machines in New York City than any place else, and more calls received by them from coin-operated telephones which can be found on nearly every street corner in town.

If they're not home much, it's surely not because their homes come cheap. At any given time, less than two per cent of the apartments in Manhattan are vacant and on any given weekend it's not uncommon for people who have been apartment-hunting for a year or more to walk the streets of desirable neighborhoods knocking on random doors in hopes that someone living there might be thinking about moving soon. The answer is usually "no," but that doesn't discourage them.

Because there is a shortage, rents are high. Depending on the desirability of the neighborhood, a $600-a-month apartment is a rare bargain and two small rooms could easily cost twice that much. Rents are usually quoted on a per-room basis, but because of a law that limits the size of increases in rent when new leases are signed, one-room apartments, called "studios," sometimes cost more than two-bedroom units in the same building. The reason is that smaller apartments get new tenants more often and more new leases mean more periodic increases in the rent.

One of the reasons for the shortage is that a huge number of New York apartment buildings have "gone co-op"–which means that the owners have sold them apartment-by-apartment to their tenants or to outsiders. In that way, New Yorkers have gotten to share one of the basic American dreams: owning their own home. But they pay a high price for the privilege. The value of a typical one-bedroom apartment in a Manhattan high-rise building is about $200,000. In lesser cities that kind of money would buy a mansion. And in lesser cities a mansion bought with that kind of money would be all yours to do with as you please. But a Manhattan cooperative apartment isn't the same thing as a mansion in Mason City, Iowa. Buying it usually involves the same down payment and the same agonizing negotiations with a bank to convince them that you are a solid citizen worthy of borrowing money at 20 per cent interest. But the similarity ends there. In New York you have to be scrutinized by the co-op board, a body made up of other people who own apartments in the building you've chosen. They usually take the selection of new neighbors very seriously. In two celebrated cases, former President Richard Nixon didn't pass muster with the board of a Fifth Avenue building and Gloria Vanderbilt, a person who could surely afford the mortgage payments, was denied the right to live under the same roof with the people who live in an elegant East Side building.

Co-op owners need to budget themselves for more than mortgage payments. There's an added monthly cost called "maintenance." The amount is set by the board and is based on the costs of running the building. There are heating and lighting bills to think about, a staff to be paid. In buildings with 24-hour doormen and elevator operators, the payroll can be steep. In older buildings or newer ones that are poorly built, lots of money needs to be collected from all the owner-tenants to keep the place ship-shape. There are taxes to be paid, and insurance. If someone in the building decides it would be nice to have heating elements installed in the building marquee to make winter comings and goings more pleasant, everyone in the building pays for it as long as the board agrees it's a good idea.

The result is that maintenance charges are subject to change and it's possible that people living in a co-op building could get a letter tomorrow morning that their monthly bill is going to be increased by $200 a month, effective right away, because the board had a meeting last night and decided that is the way it has to be.

Naturally, a co-op owner has the right to move out in the face of such a development. It's a free country, after all. But to move you first have to sell the apartment and to sell it you have to find a buyer the board will approve. While you're looking it's probably a good idea to stay away from the likes of Gloria Vanderbilt or Richard Nixon.

When the former president was told he wasn't welcome as the owner of a co-op apartment, he took the alternative of buying an entire house. The neighborhood he chose was on the East Side of Manhattan where at the time the lowest price for what they would call a "handyman's special" in suburban communities was one million dollars. The "value" has gone up considerably since then and the cost of a four-storey townhouse in any desirable Manhattan neighborhood is well over two million dollars and there are buyers waiting in line.

What you get for your investment in a New York rowhouse is often the chance to become a landlord and produce some income to help offset the monthly payments.

In the nineteenth century everyone in New York lived in four-storey houses except the very poor and newly-arrived immigrants who lived in tenement buildings. Because those multi-unit buildings were associated with the lower classes, it wasn't until after the Civil War that middle- and upper-class people took to the idea of "flats," and the early examples were designed to include all the amenities people expected in private homes.

Though they look different, the charming little houses in Greenwich Village were built on the same basic plan as the later palaces on the Upper East Side. The first floor was built up off the ground following a custom established by the first settlers from Holland who couldn't help worrying about floods. The floor was reached by a set of outside steps called a "stoop" after the Dutch word for step. Under the steps there was an entrance to a ground level floor that had a kitchen in front and a laundry room in the rear. The kitchen was placed there as a convenience to the grocer and butcher who could make deliveries without actually intruding on a family's living space. The laundry was done in the back as a convenience to the maid who had to get the water to do the washing from a well in the back yard.

Most ninetenth century New York families had at least one servant, usually a maid, because there were so many young immigrants who were as grateful for the job as for a place to live. The servants shared quarters with the young children of the family on the top floor under the roof. The floor just beneath it contained two bedrooms. The owner of the house and his wife took the back bedroom for themselves because it was quieter and overlooked the garden. The front bedroom was reserved for the older generation, the parents of the owner or some other relative, who were probably deaf and didn't mind traffic noises in the street outside.

The floor reached from the stoop was the parlor floor and every early New York house had two parlors. The one in front was kept neat and tidy as a place to entertain friends and neighbors who usually dropped in without notice back in those days before there was a telephone. The back parlor with its view of the back yard was reserved for family evenings at home and, though less elegant, was usually much more cozy and comfortable.

Though all eighteenth and nineteenth century New York houses were simple wood frame buildings, often faced with brick, all of them are loosely called "brownstones" today. The term comes from a type of sandstone common in the New Jersey hills. After the first brownstone-faced house, the rectory of the Church of the Ascension, was built on West 10th Street in 1840, the material became all the rage. It was soft enough to be easily cut and stone yards in New Jersey were kept busy for the next sixty years pre-fabricating balustrades, ornate lintels to grace windows and doorways, and entire facades for elaborate Anglo-Italian town houses which became the last word in private housing in New York both literally and figuratively.

There are about 400 of these "true brownstones" left in

Greenwich Village today, including the one at 6 Saint Luke's Place where Mayor Jimmy Walker lived from the time he was five years old. Though "Gentleman Jim's" father was a doctor, their neighbors, by and large, were middle-class tradespeople back in 1886 when the Walkers moved in. Their lives generally fell into a comfortable routine, the highpoint of the week being a stroll or a drive through the new Central Park which had been formally opened in the 1860s. In the years before that the most popular Sunday afternoon excursions were to a park that wasn't even in New York City. It was a place called "The Elysian Fields" across the Hudson River in Hoboken, New Jersey.

The park had been created by Colonel John Stevens, founder of the Stevens Institute of Technology, which still overlooks the river near the former site of his park. Stevens owned just about all of Hoboken in those days and he was eager to see it developed. As an encouragement for potential builders and buyers, he instituted New York City's first Hudson River ferry in 1811. It ran from the end of Barclay Street to Hoboken. The problem was that nobody wanted to go to Hoboken. Stevens solved that by turning a portion of his own estate into a public park.

The main event for visitors was lining up for hours for a chance to ride on the Colonel's private railroad, a little train that took seven passengers at a time on a circular route through the park. It was the first and only railroad in the United States whose train was pulled by a steam engine rather than horses.

But the park itself was the real attraction. Mrs. Trollope, the great English chronicler, hopped the ferry in 1832 and came back very impressed. "It is hardly possible to imagine a place of greater attraction," she wrote. "A broad belt of light underwood and flowering shrubs, studded at intervals with lofty forest trees, runs two miles along a cliff which overhangs the matchless Hudson. Sometimes it feathers the rocks down to its very margin and at others leaves a pebble shore, just rude enough to break the gentle waves and makes a music which mimics softly the loud chorus of the ocean. Through this beautiful wood, a broad, well-gravelled terrace is led past every point which can exhibit the scenery to advantage. Narrower and wilder paths diverge at intervals, some into the deeper shadows of the woods, some shelving gradually to the pretty coves below. The price of entrance to this little Eden is the six cents you pay at the ferry."

New Yorkers today find it tough to believe that Mrs. Trollope's Eden could possibly be Hoboken, New Jersey, even though the city has become immensely popular with people looking for good housing at a fraction of Manhattan's real estate prices.

What God and man created together on the cliffs of Hoboken, man took it upon himself to do in 1858 when architect Calvert Vaux and his friend from Staten Island, Frederick Law Olmstead, submitted what they called "The Greensward Plan" and won a design competition for the creation of a huge park at the northern edge of the settlement in Manhattan.

The area that had been selected for this "Central Park" was a mess in the 1850s when the City bought the land. It was studded with boulders and meandering streams. It was littered with squatters' shacks and little farms. In the middle of it all, where the Great Lawn is today, north of 81st Street, was a huge reservoir that had outlived its usefulness but represented a big saving in land-acquisition costs.

Olmstead and Vaux proposed tearing it all apart and starting over. Near the present corner of 59th Street and Fifth Avenue they said they would convert a dry creek bed into a pretty pond. A little further north and west, where the rock outcrops were formidable, they decided they'd get rid of the rocks and replace them with a meadow which would even have grazing sheep. Up at 74th Street, they would, they said, turn a stream into a lake. It would be a perfect terminus for the broad Mall they had planned just east of the Sheep Meadow. To give strollers the impression that the 840-acre park was bigger, they planned a few little tricks to fool the eye. One of them was to build the miniature Belvedere Castle on an axis with the Mall at the top of a rock outcrop six blocks away. Because of its small size and massive proportions it would look more like it was six miles away. Explaining the creation of the lake, Vaux wrote: "Fifty feet of water will give an idea of distance and of difficulty in passing it greater than 500 feet of ground will."

The whole project was the result of a dream by poet William Cullen Bryant, who was connected with the *New York Post* in those days and used its pages to share the dream with his neighbors. He was enthusiastically joined by authors George Bancroft and Washington Irving. Together they were able to convince the City Fathers it was a dream well worth dreaming. Before they were through, Central Park would cost more than $300 million, translated into today's dollars. But there is not a man, woman or child in the City of New York today who would not agree it was worth every penny.

The builders had their work cut out for them. It would be an awesome engineering feat even today. In the middle of the nineteenth century dynamite hadn't been invented yet, not to mention jackhammers, bulldozers and dumptrucks. All they had was black powder explosives to blast the rocks, and human brawn and horses to haul the debris away. The lakes and new streams had to be dug with picks and shovels. Thousands of trees had to be planted by hand.

The size of the labor force varied during the ten years it took to do the job. In 1862, when 74,370 trees and shrubs were planted, 3,800 men were kept busy, as were 400 horses. In that year alone they exploded 250,000 pounds of black powder.

Altogether 3,583,128 cubic yards of stone and dirt were moved to create the seemingly natural setting that became Central Park. And except for some encroachments like the ever-expanding backside of the Metropolitan Museum of Art, the park looks very much the same today as it did when the first bicycle riders began appearing there in the 1890s. Early users of the park never dreamed about skateboards and blaring radios, but in the 1870s they did a lot of complaining about millionaires like Leonard Jerome and August Belmont who used the park's drives as racecourses to get their horses warmed up for the big races they staged on the wide avenues of Harlem.

Visitors to the city, and even some New Yorkers themselves, miss the experience of Central Park because they've been told it isn't safe to go there. Statistically, it's one of the safer areas in a city that is itself safer than a dozen other smaller cities in the United States. To be sure, there are people everywhere who will prey on other people they consider vulnerable. The myth about Central Park being a hotbed of muggers and other anti-social characters probably comes from the fact that it is such a natural sylvan setting. People instinctively feel safer in natural surroundings than on a city street and every time that instinct is challenged, it is noticed more. People who choose to believe that the park is best avoided on a warm spring day when the lawns are covered with daffodils, or a crisp fall day when the elms along the Mall turn a wonderful shade of yellow, are missing out on one of the best things about New York.

The urban historian Henry Hope Reed once wrote that "Central Park is the greatest single improvement made in any American city in the course of the nation's history. No other work of art . . . has had such influence; only the national Capitol building in Washington has had more. From Central Park have sprung most major urban parks in the United States." Paul Goldberger, the architecture critic of *The New York Times*, has ranked Central Park among the top ten architectural achievements in the city's history.

Possibly the number one architectural achievement in the history of the world is the Manhattan skyline. It is a dream landscape that undulates from the towers of the financial district to the inspiring midtown mix of skyscrapers and on to the uptown apartment spires.

The first skyscrapers were built in Chicago on essentially swampy land but when the art came to New York, builders chose to anchor their towers to the solid rock that exists close to the surface from the tip of the Battery to about Canal Street and then emerges again at about 34th Street. The area in the middle, especially around Greenwich Village, is essentially marshy and criss-crossed by underground streams. The early tower builders avoided the problems of such terrain with the result that the major commercial centers leapfrogged some neighborhoods.

The same problem was considered when the first subway was built in 1904. The route ran from City Hall to the Upper West Side near Columbia University. The shortest line would have been straight up Broadway, but the engineers chose to run their line along the present route of the Lexington Avenue IRT. When they got to 42nd Street, they turned abruptly west, where the Times Square-Grand Central Shuttle runs today, and then continued on north when they hit Broadway.

The earliest skyscrapers were built near the southern end of that first subway line in the City Hall neighborhood, and the queen of them all, the Woolworth Building at 233 Broadway, just across the street from the Mayor's office, was the tallest building in the world from the day it opened in 1913 until the Chrysler Building was finished in 1930. At that time another tower at 40 Wall Skeet was also under construction and its promoters were telling the world that they were about to capture the title of tallest building in the world. The Chrysler people out-foxed them by adding a long slender spire to its graceful rounded top which made it 1,047 feet high and gave it the tallest title until the 1,472-foot Empire State Building was finished in 1931.

The Empire State held the world's record for tallness until the 1970s, when the twin towers of the World Trade Center pushed it down not once, but twice. The Trade Center towers were dedicated on April 5,1973 but less than one month later they became the second (and third) tallest buildings in the world when a Chicago upstart called the Sears Tower topped out at 104 feet higher.

Back in the late 1940s, the architect and city planner Le Corbusier said that the New York skyline was "a catastrophe," but even from the point of view of his severe taste he had to admit it "a beautiful and worthy catastrophe." Noting that at that time the city as a vertical organism was not much more than twenty years old, he was enthusiastic about the idea that "New York has such courage and enthusiasm that everything can be begun again, sent back to the building yard and made into something still greater, something mastered!"

In 1963 many New Yorkers began hanging their heads in shame over their penchant for destroying the old to make way for the new, after the building that had housed Pennsylvania Station since 1910 was torn down to make way for a much less elegant, or useful, railroad station; an office tower that ignored its street address by calling itself "Penn Plaza" and a building resembling a bass drum turned over on its side that is home to The Madison Square Garden Center. It became the fourth site of The Garden, the first having been a converted car barn, that had served the Hudson and Harlem Railroad over on Madison Square at 26th Street and Madison Avenue. The version of Madison Square Garden the latest one replaced, at Eighth Avenue and 50th Street, is still nothing more than a parking lot after twenty years.

When Penn Station disappeared, New Yorkers began asking themselves if it was such a smart idea to send the City's fine old buildings "back to the building yard." The result was a strong Landmarks Preservation law that helps protect the exteriors of important buildings and even some entire neighborhoods. The effort, and some of its results, gave a boost to other cities who saw the wisdom of "recycling" old buildings rather than tearing them down.

It also produced a wave of nostalgia and a longing for "the good old days." But how good were they?

Back in the 1880s after they arrested a small-timer named Piker Ryan, police found a price list in his pocket that ranged from a two dollar fee for a simple punching to double that much for blackening both eyes, to twenty-five dollars to stab someone. He really was a piker. A few years later the city's huge underworld came under the control of a character named Monk Eastman, whose neck and face carried a dozen or more scars from knife wounds. He liked to tell people that he had been shot so often that he had to make allowances for the bullets in his body when he weighed himself. Ambulance drivers called the emergency room at Bellevue Hospital "The Eastman Pavilion." By the turn of the century he was the undisputed king of the underworld, controlling literally hundreds of people on the streets picking pockets, snatching handbags and generally keeping the citizenry on edge while keeping rival gangs at bay. It was the high point of gang control of the city, a virtual reign of terror that had begun just before the Civil War and didn't end until the early 1930s, when the LaGuardia landslide in the mayoral election put Tammany Hall out of business once and for all and removed the likes of Monk Eastman from behind their political protection.

But if the city wasn't nearly as safe in "the good old days," was it more fun?

There is no denying they knew how to have a good time in the years between the Civil War and World War I. In the 1860s Mark Twain grumbled that "the city has grown too large." In 1868 a French journalist reported "About 20 theaters, including minstrel halls, are open to the public every night and the opera and the drama are there interpreted in divers pleasing ways to suit all tastes. As regards drinking saloons, their number is beyond calculation."

During the same period an English journalist ventured out to

Coney Island and reported: "They spread out over the four miles of sand strip with bands of music in full blast. Countless vehicles are moving; all the miniature theaters, minstrel shows, merry-go-rounds, Punch and Judy enterprises, fat women, big snakes, giant, dwarf and midget exhibitions, circuses and menageries, swings, flying horses and fortune-telling shops are open; and everywhere a dense but good-humored crowd, sightseeing, drinking beer and swallowing clam chowder."

It was the era of Diamond Jim Brady and "The" Mrs. Astor, of opulent banquets in restaurants like Delmonicos and Sherry's and feasts in Broadway lobster palaces like Rector's and Shanley's.

Looking back on it, it does seem like fun and, as always, the most fun was right here in New York City.

But it was also the time when newspaperman Jacob Riis took a hard look at the immigrant neighborhoods on the Lower East Side and found that there were 330,000 people per square mile "content to live in pigsties submitting to robbery at the hands of the rent collector without a murmer."

But in spite of what the nostalgists say, New York is probably a better place right now than it has been at any time in its history. The streets are safer, and, yes, even less congested than they were a hundred years ago. The food is better and more varied. And so is the entertainment. The best part is that it is still changing. It is still, Landmark Law or no, the only city in the world that tears itself down every ten years and builds a new city. It is the only place on earth where a native can go off on a two-week vacation and find his neighborhood changed when he gets back. It is the only place on earth that can say it is all things to all people and mean it.

After he moved to New York in the 1960s, the Irish poet, playwright and institution, Brendan Behan said: "We don't come to a city to be alone, and the test of a city is the ease with which you can see and talk to the people. A city is a place where you are least likely to get a bite from a wild sheep and I'd say New York is the friendliest city I know."

Almost anyone who's never been to New York thrives on myths like the one that says New Yorkers aren't friendly. "People live in those big apartment houses for years," they tell you, "and never get to know their next-door neighbor. You could die there and nobody would care." The fact is that most New Yorkers do know their neighbors and many of them know as much about their neighbors as anybody in any small town where all the neighbors are often related to each other. The difference is that when space is limited, people have a tendency to respect each other's space. New Yorkers are very good at that, but they do care about each other.

The city is broken down into convenient neighborhoods and anybody who has lived in one for more than a few weeks is probably on a first-name basis with the dry-cleaner, the news stand operator, the supermarket checkout clerk. They have genuine sympathy for the shoe repair man whose landlord has just raised his rent to $2,500 a month. They have their favorite neighborhood restaurants where they know they'll meet good friends on evenings when cooking doesn't seem like the perfect ending to a busy day. When they're out jogging or walking the dog it's inevitable that they'll stop for a minute or two to have a chat with a neighbor about what's going to happen to that expensive storefront now that the shoemaker has moved out and the conversation will probably lead to information about where to get their running shoes repaired now that he's gone.

Out-of-towners get a taste of New York friendliness, and pride, simply by standing on a midtown corner with a confused look. Even native New Yorkers who seem not to know where they're going will find themselves surrounded by people eager to help them. Anyone who stands on a New York street studying a guide book or a map is certain to be approached with an offer of help. Sometimes the advice is wrong, of course; even the natives don't always know that the number four bus on Madison Avenue will eventually get you all the way uptown to the Cloisters or that the best way to get from Grand Central Terminal to Penn Station is to walk over to Fifth Avenue and take the same number four bus to the other end of the line.

Though public transportation can get you anywhere you want to go in New York City, the best way to see it and capture its spirit is on foot. There are those who live in New York who still don't know that, but during a recent transit strike thousands found out and since then the best way to spot a real New Yorker is to look for someone smartly dressed but wearing sneakers. Young women executives with trim skirts and blazers and with glasses casually perched on top of their heads usually have an extra tote bag added to the soft briefcase they always carry to accommodate their high-heeled shoes. The male executives always wear three-piece suits, of course, an interesting contrast to their sneakers.

What makes walking an adventure is the unbelievable variety of people and street scenes. On the Upper East Side, the folks who run the string of boutiques along Madison Avenue thoughtfully change their window displays once a week on the average. If your route takes you through the Garment Center, on Seventh Avenue below 42nd Street, you find many of the 300,000 people who work in the neighborhood at work on the street pushing bolts of cloth on hand trucks or finished dresses on wheeled racks from one building to another. You'll see the salesmen moving their samples in waist-high wheeled suitcases, and you'll pass knots of people stopped in the middle of the sidewalk trying to find out from each other "how's business?"

On the West Side, the people will be casually-dressed in studied costumes they hope make them look "creative." On the East Side your fellow walkers will be more stylishly-dressed in outfits they know make them look "successful." Down in the financial district everybody looks successful. In Greenwich Village and SoHo everybody looks young.

But wherever you go in New York, the people are interesting, if not beautiful. There's a vitality in the city that's infectious. Even if they're not "making it," most New Yorkers are pleased to tell you that they expect they will be some day soon. And they're equally proud to tell you that making it in New York is a tough proposition. They're probably right, but at this moment there are more than seven million people taking the challenge and most of them wouldn't trade places with anyone.

New York may well be the only city in the world with a choice of 25,000 restaurants, where it's possible to have breakfast at a fine Danish restaurant, lunch at a Japanese sushi bar and dinner in an old-fashioned American place.

It's a shopper's paradise where anything that can be bought anywhere in the world is available, often at a discount. And the best part is that Manhattan itself is divided into districts that make it easier to find what you're looking for than is often possible in the arrangement of many fine department stores. Diamonds are on 47th Street, west of Fifth Avenue, or on the Bowery near Canal Street. You'll find discount hardware and hi-fi equipment down on Canal Street west of Broadway, musical instruments on Broadway above 60th Street across from Lincoln Center, Indian spices and even saris on Lexington Avenue above 23rd Street and exotic food you never dreamed existed down in Chinatown. Flowers are best bought on Sixth Avenue below 32nd Street, the best buys in cameras are in the same general area, and for fresh produce and good meat, the best place to go is Ninth Avenue above 35th Street.

But for shoppers the most fun of all is a Sunday afternoon on the Lower East Side around Orchard Street where thousands go every week to save big money on women's clothes, shoes and handbags. And the best part of that adventure is that you can go another block or two east and sample the food at a kosher Chinese restaurant or, better still, stop at an open-air shop and grab a big sour pickle right from a big oak barrel. One bite and you're in another world.

New York is another world. No other city anywhere quite compares with it. And it's getting better every day. It's a place people dream about, a place they bring their dreams to have them come true.

In fact, that's why they call New York City "The Big Apple." It all began with a dream.

Back in the days when big bands were the musical rage, they spread their fame by cruising around the country doing what they called "one-night stands." As soon as they finished playing in a place like Scranton, Pa., they'd board a bus and ride the width of Pennsylvania for their next date in Erie. The bus became their bedroom. Most tours lasted for weeks at a time and most musicians longed to sleep in a real bed.

The one place they knew that could happen was New York, where bands were playing in hotels, in theaters, in nightclubs. There were lots of big opportunities and the more they talked among themselves about it as the buses raced through the night, the more tempting it became to quit that job and take a chance with the big city. The temptation was no less irresistible than the one Eve faced back in the beginning and it wasn't long before the musicians, with their penchant for reducing everything to slang and code words, stopped talking about New York and began dreaming their dreams about "The Big Apple."

It's not just big. It's the Eighth Wonder of the World.

Previous page: an indigo sky provides an inspiring backcloth for the Statue of Liberty, which stands at the entrance of New York Harbor (these pages and overleaf). Clad in copper, the world's largest metal statue is purported to bear a resemblance to the sculptor's mother – by all accounts a strong-minded woman. Once, shipping was New York's primary reason for existence, and certainly the harbor, situated on the mouth of the Hudson River, is enormous, possessing enough depth and space to accommodate the largest ships all year round.

A 1930s hypodermic needle piercing the clouds, the Empire State Building's radio antenna mast (facing page) takes its height to an incredible 1,454 feet. Bearing the nickname of New York State, this building is the third tallest in the world. Above: the green-roofed Woolworth Building stands bright against the blank face of the World Trade Center in New York's financial district, southern Manhattan (overleaf).

With a roof not unlike that of a French chateau, the Plaza Hotel stands squarely on Fifth Avenue, commanding an enviable view over Central Park (overleaf). Its ornate architecture, distinctive beside its plainer, modern neighbors, and its wealthy clientele, help to make this prestigious hotel one of the most famous in the city. Indeed, the Plaza has been lavishly welcoming the world's rich for the best part of a century.

Above and overleaf: avenues in Central Park; green havens that seem far from those other New York avenues, lined with office blocks. Designed by Frederick Olmsted to "lift the mind out of the moods and habits created by city life," Central Park provided grazing for sheep on the Sheep Meadow until as late as 1910, and up until the Second World War, it was feasible to sleep under the stars in the park – on sweltering summer nights many would. Unfortunately, nowadays such a decision would be ill advised, but during the day the park remains an oasis for the overwrought. Right: the Beresford Apartments overlook Bethesda Fountain, which sparkles amid fall colors in Central Park.

The snow has thawed but the ice remains on a radiant day in southern Manhattan, where Brooklyn Bridge connects "the city" across the East River to one of New York's most famous boroughs. Built in 1883, this bridge holds a special place in American hearts as the first to span the East River, and a stroll along its walkway still provides one of the most awe-inspiring views of Manhattan. A short way upstream stands Manhattan Bridge (overleaf). Dating from 1909, this is as elegant a structure as Brooklyn Bridge, but one of considerably less significance in the minds of New Yorkers.

These pages and overleaf: New York City's jewel box, alive with man-made beauty early on a winter's night. From the top floors of skyscrapers, squealing brakes, the rush-hour crush of people, the police sirens and the car horns are far away. The evening is simply heralded by a silent fanfare of light that lends this, the money capital of the world, a magic that owes nothing to financial wizardry.

Constructed entirely of steel, glass and fine Vermont marble, the Secretariat Building, the United Nations headquarters on Manhattan's First Avenue, was designed under the direction of the American architect Wallace K. Harrison. Beautifully understated or devastatingly plain, depending on one's view of modernist architecture, the tower was in use by 1950. Technically, the U.N. complex is no longer part of the United States; like the Vatican, it has legal territoriality – a tiny "state within a state," it even prints its own stamps. Prior to development, the land was covered with slums and breweries, but upon its designation as the organization's site, a complete renovation of the area ensued. Overlooked by the Chrysler Building and the Empire State Building, an equestrian statue entitled "Peace" now stands in the U.N. gardens (overleaf) where once there were slaughter houses.

"Prometheus, teacher in every art, brought the fire that hath proved to mortals a means to mighty ends" reads the inscription on the wall behind the gilded statue of Prometheus outside the RCA Building. The latter, which has been described as "the most civilized and urbane skyscraper in the world," stands sentinel over a sunken plaza used as an ice rink in winter and a restaurant, thick with sunshades (overleaf), in summer. This skyscraper and plaza form the centerpiece of the Rockefeller Center Area, a group of nineteen buildings used mostly for business. The ground rent for the twenty acres they occupy is nearly $10 million a year and fills the coffers of Columbia University, which owns the site.

Upon its installation, this fifteen-foot-tall statue of "Atlas Bearing the Heavens" (above) was picketed for its supposed resemblance to Mussolini. Designed by Lee Lawrie in 1937, the bronze stands outside the International Building of the Rockefeller Center. Facing page: gloriously Gothic, nineteenth-century St. Patrick's Cathedral on Fifth Avenue, one of the loveliest – and one of the largest – churches on that thoroughfare.

Above: looking a little like a Cossack's hat banded with a ribbon of light, the Guggenheim Museum is one of New York's most architecturally distinctive. Particularly pleasing inside, where the floor ascends in a spiral around a simple red mobile (left), the museum houses an extensive collection of modern art, ranging from Impressionist work to that of the present day. Sadly, Solomon Guggenheim, the copper magnate who commissioned Frank Lloyd Wright to design the building, died before the work even began, but his collection forms the core of the exhibits here.

Above: Toulouse-Lautrec, Gauguin and Van Gogh stand their ground beside more recent work (top) in Manhattan's Museum of Modern Art. This museum embraces all visual arts, from architecture through painting to photography, cinema and graphic design, and boasts a fine sculpture garden as well. Facing page: a wall of water on Fifth Avenue beside one of the world's finest museums, the Metropolitan Museum of Art.

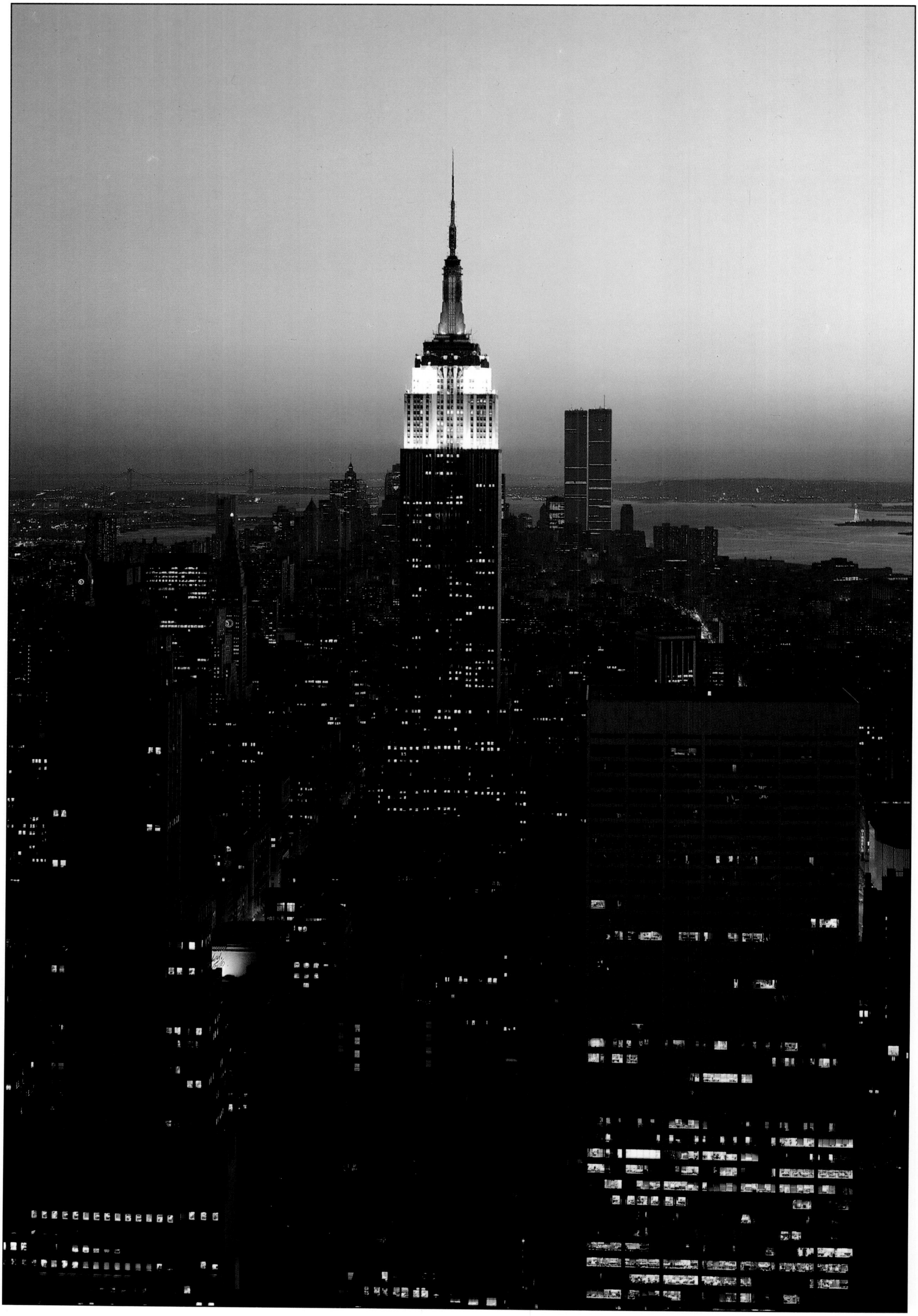

Completed during the Depression, the Empire State Building (these pages) suffered the ignominy of the nickname "the Empty State Building" throughout the 1930s; it was only after the Second World War that the great tower – then the tallest in the world – was fully utilized. Overleaf: part of the 360°-view to be had from the tower's observation deck, a view that can stretch for eighty miles from atop this, the "Eighth Wonder of the World."

At a quarter of a mile high, the World Trade Tower Observation Deck (above and right) offers a panorama that is breathtaking – sometimes literally so on the rooftop promenade, the highest outdoor observation platform on earth. Certainly the mirrored corridor (above right) of the Empire State Building is not for acrophobes as it is impossible to turn away from the view. Overleaf: rain clouds soften the severity of the World Trade Center towers, the elongated cubes that comprise the second highest building in the world. Construction began in 1966 and the Center was dedicated just seven years later to provide the Port Authority of New York and New Jersey with new headquarters.

Top: battered but unbowed, New York cabs line up outside Park Avenue's Grand Hyatt Hotel near Grand Central Station. This large, thirty-story hotel contains nearly 1,500 rooms and was formerly the Commodore Hotel. Above: Helmsley Palace Hotel on Madison Avenue, Manhattan, where the entrance and public rooms are part of the restored Villard Houses of 1884, Italian Renaissance buildings modeled after Rome's Palazzo della Cancelleria and built by newspaper owner Henry Villard. Facing page: flags fly over the crowds outside Cartier's on Fifth Avenue.

Below: shoppers on Fifth Avenue attract a legion of cabs. Fifth Avenue is synonymous with luxury the world over; not only does it contain some of America's finest department stores, such as Macy's and Bloomingdale's, it is also the address of many of New York's richest residents. Facing page: tourists pausing for breath on the steps of Fifth Avenue's St. Patrick's Cathedral, reminiscent of Cologne Cathedral, Germany.

Away from the more famous sights, the tall, but not very tall, buildings, the dominating advertizing hoardings and the higgledy-piggledy shop signs at the intersection of 42nd Street and 8th Avenue (facing page) are typical of New York. Top: bargain clothes stores display their wares like flags on Orchard Street, Lower East Side, and (above) cars, people and shop signs crowd Chinatown, south Manhattan.

These pages: flag-flying patriotism on Fifth Avenue, where it appears to be de rigueur to hang the Stars and Stripes from each storefront, and (above) the cast iron clock at the intersection of Fifth Avenue and 44th Street, which has saved many a Grand Central commuter from missing his train. This clock is one of a handful of rare survivors from the turn of the century and New Yorkers regularly set their watches by it.

The lights of passing cars leave trails like tracer bullets in Times Square (these pages). At night, the square's neon signs come into their own, enjoining the stroller to buy cameras, sound systems and soft drinks for his entertainment, while beneath these glittering hoardings, the cinemas and theaters attempt to draw his attention to new releases and Broadway productions. During the day, it can all look rather tawdry and untidy (overleaf) – only night brings the glamor the Square's reputation demands.

A baby grand piano and a photograph of England's Windsor Castle lend touches of old-world charm to the glittering atrium of the Citicorp Center in midtown Manhattan. Built on Lexington Avenue in 1977 to a height of 900 feet, the Center is the world's second tallest multi-use building and also one of its most distinctive. Its abruptly angled roof, a striking feature of its exterior, was designed for solar panels, though these have yet to be installed.

With everything from canned iced tea to fruit punch offered on a soft drink vendor's cart (above), and doughnuts (left) and pretzels (above left) available fresh from a wayside stall, fast food in New York is a cheap and convenient way to assuage a thirst or an appetite. If the street is not found to be conducive to bon appetit, however, the Sign of the Dove Inn (overleaf) on Third Avenue is well-equipped to provide the diner with a superb meal in far more sophisticated surroundings

Above: stone vases and white shutters lend a nineteenth-century air to Grove Court, a select residential area in Greenwich Village. The Village, whose heart lies in Washington Square Park (top) at the end of Fifth Avenue, is associated with artists, especially writers and painters, and many of America's finest have lived here. Facing page: bamboo flourishes in the covered plaza of the IBM Building on East 57th Street.

Red, the Chinese color for good luck, predominates on shop signs in Doyers Street, part of Manhattan's Chinatown. The Chinese arrived in New York in substantial numbers after the War of Secession, and initially the area was rife with Tong gangsters: there were so many shootings at the T-junction between Pell Street and Doyers Street that for a time it was known as "the Bloody Corner." By 1910 things had simmered down, and today this city within a city is perhaps best known to non-Chinese for its fabulous wealth of restaurants, and the wonderful dragons on parade during its annual New Year spectacular. Overleaf: the lights of the World Trade Center pale into insignificance beside a harbor firework display, part of New York's Fourth of July celebrations.

Right: their mouths agape as if they were ever hungry, stone lion heads top the classical frontage of the New York Stock Exchange on Broad Street. Inside, on the dealers' floor (above), the city boys jostle for the core of the "Big Apple" – money. Millions of dollars are traded in stocks and shares here every weekday, requiring both flair and courage to juggle deftly with such enormous sums. Certainly, amid such frenetic activity, no dealer worth his salary bothers with waste baskets. Overleaf: metalwork of almost lace-like intricacy on Queensboro Bridge, whose architect, Henry Hornbostel, feared that so much cast iron resembled a "blacksmith's shop."

Above: laser-like beams of red and white light – rush hour traffic in motion – direct the eye to the Helmsley Building, a tower which seems slim in front of the broad expanse of the Pan Am Building. Facing page and overleaf: the windows of a Manhattan skyscraper resemble matchbox-sized television screens. As twilight turns to night, such "light boxes" are all that remain to indicate the shape of downtown buildings.

The Hudson River smooths the circuit-board complexity of Manhattan office lights into simple, fluid bands of color. Viewed like this — simplified by the night into blocks of black and brilliant shades of aquamarine — New York is a dazzlingly beautiful city. Overleaf: the tower of the Metropolitan Life Insurance Company Headquarters glows like a gas flame as a simmering twilight settles over downtown Manhattan.

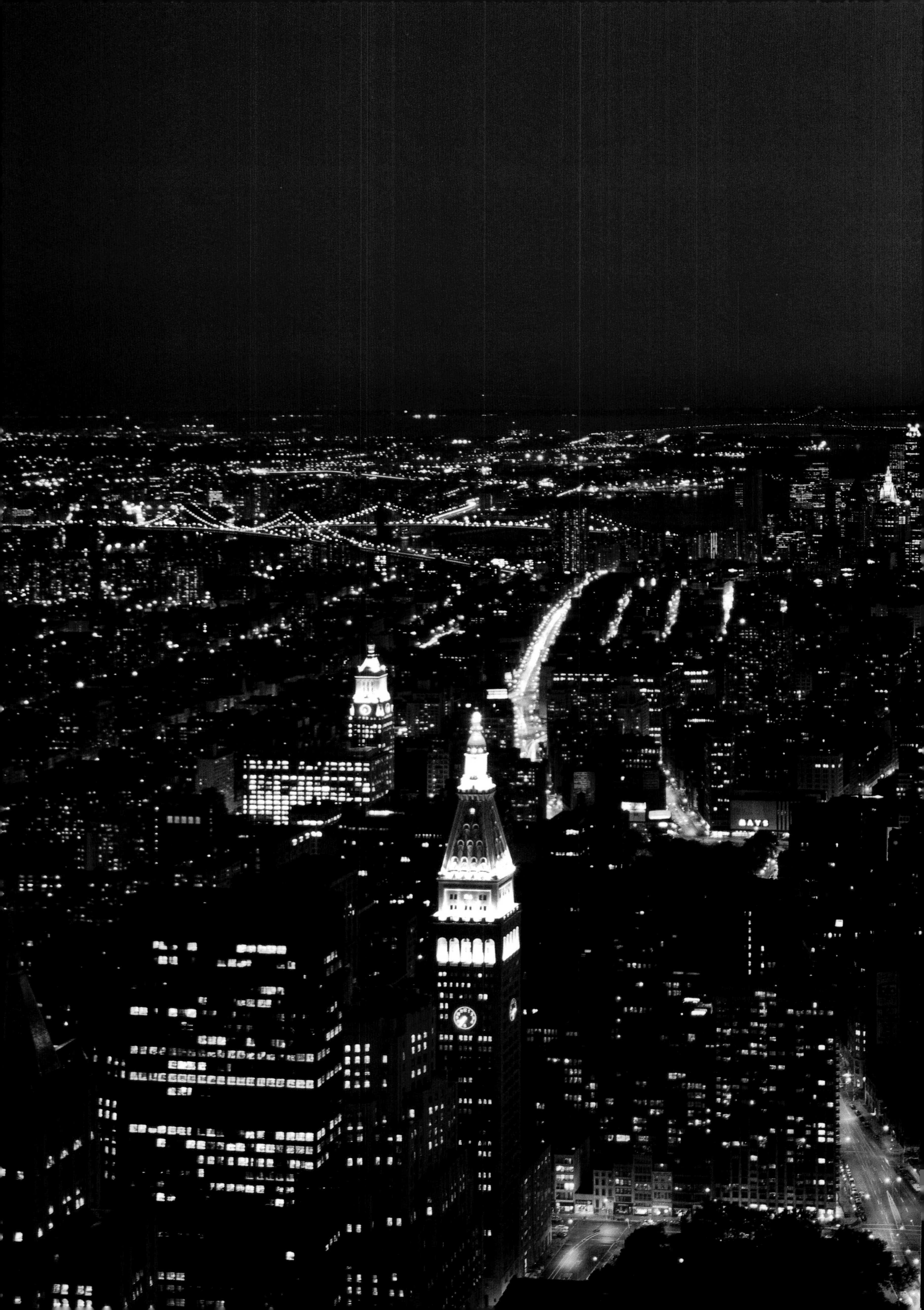

Above: streaming towards the sky, the strong lines of the World Trade Center towers are distorted by their reflections in another building, but still the eye is drawn ever upwards. The design of these two great, 110-story hexahedrons was a radical departure from the conventional steel-frame concepts of the past, as the walls of these towers are load-bearing, instead of being merely glass skins covering central supports. This allows the interior to be free of columns, but means that the Center's windows are unusually narrow. Right: clouds reflected in a tower of concertina-like design on Fifth Avenue, and (overleaf) central Manhattan. If skyscrapers symbolize ambition, New York is the most ambitious city in the world.

South Street Seaport Museum comprises a collection of vintage sailing vessels beside Brooklyn Bridge. Alongside these ships, the museum has also preserved eighteenth- and nineteenth-century buildings and piers within a thirty-three-acre area, and is completely pedestrianized so that cars cannot intrude into this idealized atmosphere of the past. In contrast, neighboring Fulton Fish Market is a bustling, strong-smelling reminder of old New York – there has been a fish market at this location in southern Manhattan since the 1600s. Overleaf: Fourth of July celebrations on the East River bring together craft as diverse as motor launches and sailing ships to fly the flag in front of a wall of Manhattan skyscrapers.

Above: the big wedge of the Citicorp Center, shimmering in the aluminum skin that stretches between the building's layers of glittering windows. These windows appear to have the slimmest of vertical frames, so from a distance the tower (overleaf) seems to consist of levels of light as much as of tiers of metal. Facing page: at dusk the triangular Flatiron Building seems to move into the illuminated fork of Broadway and Fifth Avenue like the prow of an ocean liner leaving a wake of phosphorescence over a dark sea.

112

On a bracing, blue-gray day in winter the colors of Brooklyn Bridge's dignified columns are echoed in the dual pillars of the World Trade Center. Such is the incredible height of these modern towers that from this approach they appear to be only a few hundred yards away from the shoreline of the East River, yet, in reality, they stand on the opposite side of Manhattan (overleaf).

Alongside wedges, glass boxes, Gothic decoration and Art Deco, the Manhattan skyline can now boast oval skyscrapers and towers with Chippendale-like pediments. New York was ever the "city of the new," and true originality in architecture is highly prized here. Towers at this density (overleaf), however, have the disadvantage of making the streets between them dark canyons of concrete, since these tall buildings throw permanent shadows. A true New Yorker, though, will happily forgive these side effects of height to be surrounded by architecture of such imaginative grandeur.

Perhaps no other statue in history has meant so much to so many. Upon seeing the Statue of Liberty for the first time, one nineteenth-century immigrant remembered "She was beautiful in the early morning light. Everybody was crying. The whole boat bent towards her because everybody went out." Overleaf: dawn in an almost deserted Manhattan, where only that grand old lady, Brooklyn Bridge, is still wearing a necklace of lights from the night before. Like all cities, New York needs its people before it can shine.

INDEX